Kangaroos · Canguros

ALICE TWINE

TRADUCCIÓN AL ESPAÑOL:
José María Obregón

PowerKiDS & **Editorial Buenas Letras**™
press
New York

Published in 2008 by The Rosen Publishing Group, Inc.
29 East 21st Street, New York, NY 10010

First Edition

Editor: Amelie von Zumbusch
Book Design: Julio Gil
Photo Researcher: Nicole Pristash

Photo Credits: Cover, p. 1, 5, 7, 9, 11, 19, 24 (top left, top right, bottom right) Shutterstock.com; p. 13 © www.istockphoto.com/Phil Morley; pp. 15, 23, 24 (bottom left) © www.istockphoto.com/Susan Flashman; p. 17 © www.istockphoto.com/Eric Gevaert; p. 21© www.istockphoto.com/Michelle Gustavson.

Cataloging Data

Twine, Alice.
  Kangaroos–Canguros / Alice Twine; traducción al español: José María Obregón. — 1st ed.
     p. cm. — (Baby animals–Animales bebé).
  ISBN-13: 978-1-4042-7684-0 (library binding)
  ISBN-10: 1-4042-7684-X (library binding)
  1. Kangaroos—Infancy—Juvenile literature. 2. Spanish language materials.

Manufactured in the United States of America.

Websites: Due to the changing nature of Internet links, PowerKids Press and Editorial Buenas Letras have developed an online list of Web sites related to the subject of this book. This site is updated regularly. Please use this link to access the list: www.powerkidslinks.com/baby/kang/

Contents

Contenido

Do you know what this animal in its mother's **pouch** is? It is a kangaroo! Baby kangaroos are called joeys.

¿Sabes qué animal es el que se encuentra en la **bolsa** de su mamá? ¡Es un canguro bebé!

4

Kangaroos, like this joey, are known for their long legs. Kangaroos can hop as far as 30 feet (9 m) in one jump.

Los canguros son famosos por su largas patas traseras. Los canguros pueden saltar hasta 30 pies (9 m) en un salto.

6

While kangaroos have long legs, they have short **forelimbs**. Kangaroos have **claws** on both their legs and their forelimbs.

Aunque los canguros tienen largas patas traseras, sus **patas delanteras** son cortas. Los canguros tienen **garras** en las patas.

8

Kangaroos live in Australia. They live in open woodlands and grasslands.

Los canguros viven en Australia. Los canguros viven en los bosques y en los prados.

10

There are several different kinds of kangaroos. This joey is an eastern grey kangaroo.

Hay canguros de muchos tipos. Este bebé es un canguro gris oriental.

Red kangaroos live in the dry middle part of Australia. Red kangaroos are the largest kind of kangaroo.

Los canguros rojos viven en la parte central y árida de Australia. Los canguros rojos son los canguros más grandes.

14

A newborn joey crawls into its mother's pouch. Several months later, the joey looks out of the pouch for the first time.

Los canguros recién nacidos se trepan en la bolsa de su mamá. Meses más tarde, el canguro bebé se asoma por primera vez.

Joeys drink their mother's milk. Newborn joeys drink only milk, but older joeys eat grass and other plants, too.

Los canguros bebé toman leche de sus mamás. Al crecer, los canguros bebé comen hierbas y plantas.

19

Kangaroos often sleep during the day. Young joeys sleep in their mother's pouch. Older joeys sleep on the ground.

Los canguros bebé duermen mucho durante el día. Los más pequeños duermen en la bolsa de sus mamás. Los más grandes duermen en el suelo.

A joey and its mother are often part of a bigger group of kangaroos. A group of kangaroos is called a **mob**.

Muchas veces, un canguro bebé y su mamá forman parte de un grupo de canguros. A estos grupos se les llama **manadas**.

Words to Know • Palabras que debes saber

claws / (las) garras

forelimbs / (las) patas delanteras

mob / (la) manada

pouch / (la) bolsa